EXPLORE CHINA
12 KEY FACTS

by Marne Ventura

www.12StoryLibrary.com

12-Story Library is an imprint of Bookstaves.

Photographs ©: aphotostory/iStockphoto, cover, 1; shrimpo1967/CC2.0, 4; Daniel Doerfler/Shutterstock.com, 5; Valery Bocman/Shutterstock.com, 6; Chen Wu/CC2.0, 7; JesseW900/CC4.0, 8; Antilong/CC3.0, 10; JEFF WIDENER/Associated Press, 11; chung toan co/Shutterstock.com, 12; xieyuliang/Shutterstock.com, 13; junrong/Shutterstock.com, 14; EQRoy/Shutterstock.com, 15; Anirut Krisanakul/Shutterstock.com, 16; Zapp2Photo/Shutterstock.com, 17; EQRoy/Shutterstock.com, 18; PRILL/Shutterstock.com, 19; Patrick Foto/Shutterstock.com, 20; atiger/Shutterstock.com, 21; atiger/Shutterstock.com, 22; Min Jing/Shutterstock.com, 23; WHYFRAME/Shutterstock.com, 24; tongcom photographer/Shutterstock.com, 25; Chris Nener/CC2.0, 26; J. Lekavicius/Shutterstock.com, 27; Artgraphixel/Shutterstock.com 28; Nannucci/iStockphoto, 29

ISBN
978-1-63235-553-9 (hardcover)
978-1-63235-610-9 (paperback)
978-1-63235-670-3 (ebook)

Library of Congress Control Number: 2018940810

Printed in the United States of America
Mankato, MN
June, 2018

About the Cover

The Great Wall of China was built in northern China over 2,000 years ago.

Access free, up-to-date content on this topic plus a full digital version of this book. Scan the QR code on page 31 or use your school's login at 12StoryLibrary.com.

Table of Contents

China Is a Huge Country

China covers a vast area. It is the fourth-largest country in the world. It is the largest country in Asia. It has mountains, deserts, and rivers. China shares borders with 14 countries. There are islands along its coastlines. These coastlines meet the East China Sea and the South China Sea. Both seas are part of the Pacific Ocean.

The Himalayas rise in China's west.

Mountains make up one-third of the land of China. The Himalayans rise 20,000 feet (6,000 m) above sea level in the west. Mount Everest is the world's tallest mountain. It is on the border between China and Nepal.

One-fifth of China is deserts. Deserts stretch across northwestern China. The Gobi Desert runs through Mongolia and northern China.

The Yangtze is also called the Chang Jiang, for Long River.

Much of the Gobi is bare rock. The Taklamakan Desert is southwest of the Gobi. It is one of the world's biggest sandy deserts.

Thousands of rivers flow through China. The two most important are the Yellow and the Yangtze. Both start in the Tibetan Plateau. The Yellow River is the sixth longest in the world. It winds eastward through northern China to the Yellow Sea. The Yangtze River is the longest in China and third longest in the world. It flows eastward to the East China Sea.

3.7 million
Area in square miles (9.6 million km) of China.

- China is a huge country with many land types.
- Mountains are one-third of the area.
- Deserts make up one-fifth of China.
- The Yellow and Yangtze rivers flow through China.

China Has Diverse Environments

The climate in different areas of China varies. Icy winter winds blow across the deserts. Summer ocean winds in the south bring heat and rain. The weather changes with the seasons in the river valleys. In the northeast, summer is short and hot. Winter is long and chilly. The Himalayan Mountains are cold and snowy year-round.

In southern China, rainforests are home to giant pandas, tigers, monkeys, and elephants. Rare snow leopards live in Tibet. Thousands of species of fish and hundreds of types of amphibians and reptiles live in the rivers and coastal waters. Yaks and gazelle roam the grasslands between Tibet and Mongolia.

More than 30,000 plant species are native to China. Some are used to make medicine. Many serve to decorate landscapes. Some plants

Tropical rainforests can be found on Hainan Island and in Yunnan Province.

Pandas eat up to 84 pounds (38 kgs) of bamboo every day.

provide food for people. In forests and rainforests, plants are homes for wildlife.

In the north, temperatures in winter range from -4 to -40 degrees Fahrenheit (-20°C to -40°C). Sometimes snow falls on the sand dunes in the desert. In summer, the temperature in Beijing, China's capital, can be as high as 100 degrees Fahrenheit (38°C).

86

Annual temperature range in °F (48°C) between the south and north.

- China has different climates.
- A variety of animals live in China.
- There is a wide range of temperatures.

ONLY IN CHINA

Over 100 wild animal species are unique to China. The best-known is the giant panda. Pandas average 77 pounds (135 kg). They eat the leaves and shoots of bamboo trees. These bears are a symbol of the world's endangered animals. There are only about 1,500 left.

China Has a Long History

This statue of Emperor Qin stands near his tomb in the Shaanxi province.

China was one of the world's first civilizations. Due to its large size and isolation from other cultures, China developed without much outside influence.

In 221 BCE, Emperor Qin (pronounced "chin") was the first to unite the people. He began building the Great Wall to protect China from invaders. Qin's rule was followed by a series of dynasties. A dynasty is when the

4,000
Length in years of China's recorded history.

- Qin first united China.
- A series of dynasties ruled after Qin.
- People rebelled against dynastic rule in 1912.
- China is now a key player in the modern world.

same family rules over a country for a long period of time. The Han Dynasty ruled for four centuries.

In 1912, the people rebelled. Rule by dynasties ended. A new government was formed. By 1937, warlords, the Communist Party, and the Chinese Nationalist Party were all fighting for power.

A communist named Mao Zedong took over in 1949. He began the People's Republic of China. He forbade religion, private wealth, and old methods of education and farming. Schools were closed. People were forced to do work against their will. Shops and farms were taken over by the government.

When Mao died in 1976, new leaders allowed China to become modern. They let information from the Western world come into China. They allowed Chinese merchants to trade with other countries. They stopped government control of farms and shops. They let people own property.

TIMELINE

221 BCE: Qin Dynasty unites China.

207 BCE–1271 CE: A series of dynasties rules.

1271: Mongols invade and rule for 100 years.

1368: Ming Dynasty overthrows Mongols and completes Great Wall.

1912: Chinese rebel against dynastic rule.

1949: Mao creates People's Republic of China.

1976: China begins to modernize under new leaders.

2001: China joins the World Trade Organization.

2008: China hosts the 2008 Summer Olympics.

4 A Strong Central Government Rules China

A powerful government rules the People's Republic. There are four branches of government in China. They are the legislative, the executive, the judicial, and the military branches.

Most government officials belong to the Chinese Communist Party (CCP). They are appointed rather than elected. The same is true for judges in China's Supreme Court. The president of China is the head of the country, the Communist Party, and the military.

China has 23 provinces. There are also nine regions that rule themselves. Most Chinese are from the Han ethnic group. There are many other small ethnic groups, such as the Tibetans. These

Xi Jinping became president of China in 2012.

groups want more independence but are still controlled by the government.

In the late 1900s, the government named four zones where companies from other countries could set up factories and hire Chinese workers. This made it easier to trade with China. Many Chinese hoped these changes would bring a new government where people

An anonymous man blocks a column of tanks as they move toward Tiananmen Square. Today he is known as Tank Man.

could have more choices. In 1989, thousands of citizens gathered in Tiananmen Square in Beijing, China's capital city, to ask for democracy. The government responded by sending in the army. Over 1,000 people were killed and many more were arrested. Today it is still difficult for Chinese to criticize their government without being punished.

2018
Year when term limits for China's president were removed.

- China has a strong central government.
- Members of the Communist Party control China.
- China is divided into provinces.
- People asking for democracy were punished at Tiananmen Square.

THINK ABOUT IT

Members of the Communist Party are in charge of the government of China. What form of government runs your country? To which political parties do government officials belong? Read and research online to find out more.

11

China Is Important to the World Economy

The population of China is the largest on Earth. They have a huge workforce to grow crops and make products. China has many natural resources. Iron ore, coal, and oil are plentiful. Farmers in China produce much of the world's grain. Factories in China sell products to the rest of the world.

Only about 10 percent of China's land is suitable for farming. The remaining land is too dry, stony, or cold for growing crops. Despite this, China is the world's number one rice grower. It is also a major producer of wheat, corn, tobacco, soybeans, peanuts, and cotton.

Most of the workers and factories in China are in the south and east. China's important exports are textiles and clothing, machinery, food, chemicals, and electronic products. Factory workers in China make cameras, air conditioners, televisions, and toys.

Since the late 1970s, China has become a key player in the world economy. It exports products to other countries. People are leaving farms in the country to work in factories in the city. China is now one of the largest economies on Earth. Experts predict it will continue to grow at a rapid rate.

The Chinese have been growing rice for over 7,500 years.

THE DOWNSIDE TO AN UP ECONOMY

China's growing economy is both good and bad news. More Chinese than ever before earn enough to save, buy a car, or take a vacation. Millions of workers have moved to the city for better paying jobs. But many have had to leave their children behind with relatives. Cities are overcrowded. More factories cause air, water, and soil pollution.

6.9

Percent growth rate of Chinese economy in 2017.

- China has a big workforce and many natural resources.
- Chinese farms produce rice and other crops.
- Factories in China make many products.
- China's economy is growing.

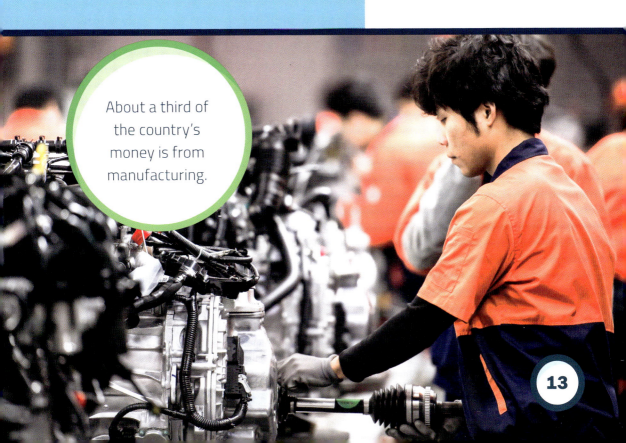

About a third of the country's money is from manufacturing.

The Government Provides Public Education

Children in China start school when they are six years old. They go to elementary school for six years, middle school for three years, and high school for three years. Students study Chinese language and literature, math, natural science, and values.

The Chinese system of reading and writing uses symbols called characters. Unlike an alphabet where letters stand for sounds, the Chinese system is made up of 60,000 characters. Learning to read and write in Chinese means memorizing thousands of symbols. Most students know 6,000 characters by the time they start high school.

The government pays for schools in big cities, but not always in rural areas. In general, children in bigger cities have a better chance of getting a good education and going to college. Students who are not going on to college get job training during high school. Those who want to go to a university must take an exam. If they pass, the government pays for their education. In exchange, the students must

agree to take a government-chosen job when they graduate.

There are six universities in China. The government runs them. Each province also has a university. There are many technical colleges. The goal of most university training is to prepare students for technical jobs. China now has the most college graduates with degrees in science and engineering.

Over 45,000 students attend Tsinghua University in Beijing, which has been ranked the best in the world for engineering.

100
Percent of 15- to 24-year-olds in China who are literate.

- The Chinese government provides public education.
- Learning to read in Chinese involves learning thousands of characters.
- Students either go to college or get job training in high school.
- There are six government-run universities in China.

THINK ABOUT IT

Which countries don't provide public education for their children? Do you think children around the world should be given a free education? Read and research online to find out more.

Chinese Inventions Are Used Worldwide

Chinese inventors made many of the things that people around the world use every day. Some of the first astronomers, mathematicians, craftsmen, scientists, and engineers were Chinese. At the start of their history, Chinese inventors were isolated from other nations. During the twentieth century, China opened factories to mass-produce and trade with Western countries.

Ancient Chinese inventors made the first gunpowder. This led to the invention of fireworks. Fireworks are a big part of Chinese holidays. In the fourth century BCE, Chinese inventors made the first compasses.

China produces 90 percent of the world's fireworks.

Medical robots provide facial recognition, patient consultation, and other services.

They used lodestone, a type of magnetic iron ore, to make a device that points south. In 105 CE, a Chinese inventor mixed wood fibers and water and pressed the material into a woven cloth. The result was the first paper.

It's not clear who invented pasta, but archaeologists found a bowl of 4,000-year-old noodles buried near a Chinese settlement. A general during the Han Dynasty came up with the wheelbarrow. Other inventions from the ancient Chinese include printing, kites, hang gliders, silk, and the seismograph, which measures earthquakes.

In 2003, China's first rocket sent a man into space. In 2008, a Chinese astronaut walked in space. The Chinese space program is now working to set up its own space station and land on the moon.

The Chinese government invests money in brain research, gene science, big data, and medical robots. They are second only to the United States in the amount they spend on scientific research.

426,000
Number of scientific publications from China in 2016.

- Many ancient Chinese inventions are now used around the world.
- The Chinese space program began in 2003.
- China funds science and technology research.

China Is Working On Its Infrastructure

Making an infrastructure work for a vast country with a huge population is a big job. Overcrowding in cities causes traffic jams, pollution, and power shortages. The government of China is working to help people travel more easily and live more comfortable lives.

In cities, people walk, ride bicycles, or take a bus to school or work.

The easiest way to travel in China outside of the city is by train. Flying is too expensive for most people. In some rural areas, the roads are not in good condition. This makes it hard to travel by car.

China is building new roads and airports. It is also building a high-speed railway network. Trains run at

The bullet train in China can travel up to 217 mph (350 km/h).

The Three Gorges Dam generates 11 times more power than the Hoover Dam in the US.

speeds of 155–217 miles per hour (250–350 km/h).

In 2006, Chinese engineers finished building the world's largest dam. The dam is in a region called the Three Gorges. The Yangtze River flows into the dam. The dam turns energy from moving water into electricity. It provides about one-tenth of China's energy. It stops flooding and saves water for farms. Building the dam displaced 1.2 million people. It also disrupted wildlife in the region.

$1 trillion

Amount of money China expects to spend on infrastructure in the coming years.

- China's size makes infrastructure a challenge.
- People in cities walk, bike, or ride the bus.
- China is building new roads, airports, and a high-speed railway.
- The Three Gorges Dam converts water to electricity.

BELT AND ROAD

In 2013, China announced a new project called the Belt and Road Initiative (BRI). China plans to use modern infrastructure to connect with 70 other countries across Asia, Africa, Europe, and Oceania. BRI will include roads, railway tracks, ports, airports, pipelines, electric grids, and fiber optic lines. China's hope is that BRI will help it play an even greater role in global affairs.

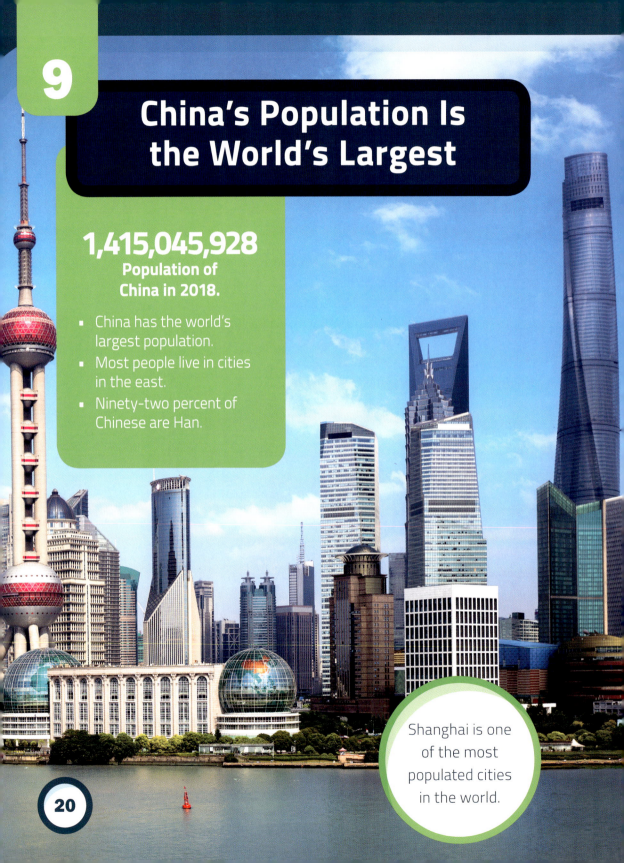

9

China's Population Is the World's Largest

1,415,045,928
Population of China in 2018.

- China has the world's largest population.
- Most people live in cities in the east.
- Ninety-two percent of Chinese are Han.

Shanghai is one of the most populated cities in the world.

More people live in China than in any other country. Most of the people live in the east. The Yangtze and Yellow River valleys are the most crowded areas. Almost 24 million people live in Shanghai. Almost 21 million live in the capital, Beijing. Over one hundred cities have a population of more than one million.

Nearly half of the people in China are between the ages of 25 and 54. About 17 percent of Chinese are under the age of 14. Thirteen percent are 15- to 24-year-olds. People older than 55 make up about 22 percent of the population.

There are 56 ethnic groups in China. Each group has its own language and traditions. More than 90 percent of the people are Han Chinese. The Han dynasty ruled China from about 206 BCE to 220 CE. Rulers expanded China's borders and created a new government system. The Hans came after the Qin. The era is called a Golden Age in Chinese history. Hans made many advances in the arts, politics, and technology.

A family takes a selfie in Shanghai.

SLOWING POPULATION GROWTH

In 1979, the Chinese government wanted to slow the growth of the country's population. They made a rule that families in cities could have only one child. At the start of 2016, a new rule was put in place. Couples are now allowed to have two children.

China Has a Rich Culture

Chinese New Year is the country's most important holiday. It starts with the first new moon of the year. The celebration lasts until the next full moon. According to ancient legend, a monster attacked villages at the start of a new year. To scare it away, people used firecrackers, fireworks, and red clothes and decorations. In modern China, people have parades, eat special foods, and spend time with family.

People in China do not have complete freedom of religion. The Chinese Communist Party (CCP) is atheist. While Mao Zedong ruled

The Chinese New Year for 2018 ushers in the Year of the Dog.

China, between 1935 and 1976, he forbade religion. After Mao, China became more modern and open to the Western world. The government loosened its control over religion. Today in China the constitution allows five mainstream religions. However, the CCP sometimes arrests or punishes religious groups who meet in public.

Food in China is as diverse as the regions and people. Rice is a staple in southern China. Dumplings and noodles are eaten in the north. People eat lots of fresh vegetables. Typical meals include chopped vegetables and bits of meat or fish. These are quickly fried in a deep pan called a wok. Then they are served over rice or noodles. Chinese people eat from bowls using chopsticks.

7

Days off given to workers during Chinese New Year.

- Chinese New Year is the biggest holiday.
- The constitution allows religion, but the Communist Party does not.
- People in China eat meat, vegetables, rice, and noodles.

THINK ABOUT IT

Do you have religious freedom? Which countries do not allow religious freedom? Read and research online to find out more.

Chinese dumplings have various fillings and can be steamed or fried.

Health Care Is a Challenge

Staying healthy is an important part of daily life in China. Many people rise early to practice an exercise called tai chi in the parks near their homes. In cities, most street markets have shops where people can get a massage. People who walk or bike to work and school get plenty of healthy exercise.

China's health care system faces a challenge in keeping up with its population. For every 2,000 hospital patients, there are only three doctors. A large part of the population is seniors who need medical care. China also has the most obese children and most diabetes patients in the world. To keep up, China has reformed its insurance program in recent years. Today 95 percent of the population has health care insurance.

Tai chi, also known as shadow boxing, is a branch of traditional Chinese martial arts.

Before 2016, the government allowed couples to have only one child. The government now lets couples have two children. Despite this, the birth rate declined in recent years. Experts say that by the end of 2035, there will be 400 million elderly people in China. This will put a strain on China's health care system. There will be too many people who need care and too few young people to enter the work force.

TRADITIONAL CHINESE MEDICINE

Chinese medicine is based on a different philosophy than Western medicine. Chinese doctors link internal organs to certain points on the person's skin. During a massage, the therapist puts pressure on those points to keep the person healthy and relaxed. Acupuncture is a Chinese treatment where needles are put into these pressure points. Other therapies include drinking herbal teas.

76

Average life expectancy in years of Chinese people today.

- Most Chinese people get lots of exercise.
- Providing health care for a large population is a challenge.
- The birth rate has declined while the number of elderly has risen.

Country and City Homes Are Different

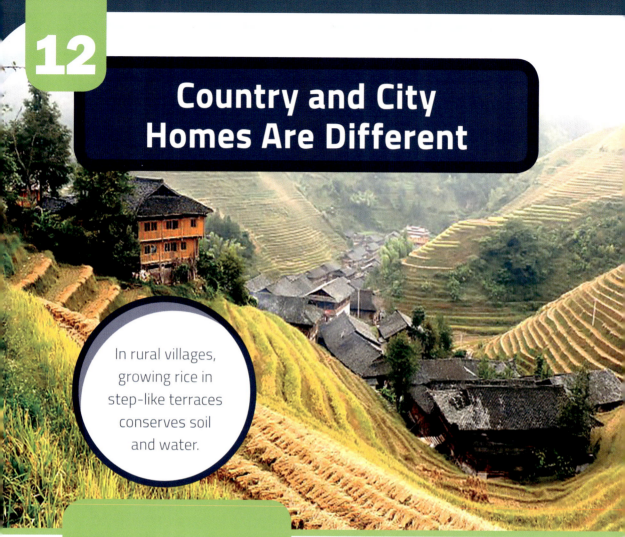

In rural villages, growing rice in step-like terraces conserves soil and water.

60

Percent of the population living in urban areas.

- Rural Chinese live in villages.
- Urban Chinese live mostly in high-rise buildings.
- China is the world's largest energy user.

Since China is such a vast and diverse country, the types of homes people live in can vary widely. In rural villages, homes are built close together. This keeps everyone near the water source, which is usually a well. In the past, it also helped people defend themselves against invaders. Rural homes are often made of sun-dried brick or pounded soil. Sometimes walls are built around the village. Farmers set up outdoor markets to sell produce. In the late 1970s, advances in farming reduced the need for workers in rural areas. Many moved to cities to work in factories. Some stayed and started small businesses.

In cities, people live in high-rise apartments. In the mid-1920s, government reforms made it possible for people in cities to buy and sell real estate. Before then, people paid rent to live in government-owned buildings.

Today 90 percent of families own their home. Usually relatives pool money to buy a home. It's normal for grandparents, parents, children, aunts and uncles to live together.

China is the world's largest energy user. The country mines and burns half of the world's coal. Since coal causes pollution, the government is pushing to use cleaner sources of energy such as natural gas. They are building more wind, solar, and hydropower plants. These sources of energy are cleaner than coal or oil and less harmful to the environment.

A typical apartment building in Shanghai.

China at a Glance

Population in 2018: 1,415,045,928

Area: 3,600,947 square miles (9,326,410 sq km)

Capital: Beijing

Largest Cities: Shanghai, Guangzhou, Beijing, Shenzhen, Wuhan

Flag:

Official Language: Mandarin

Currency: Official name is Renminbi, which means "the people's currency." Also called Yuan, which is the name of a unit of the currency.

What people who live in China are called: Chinese

Where in the World?

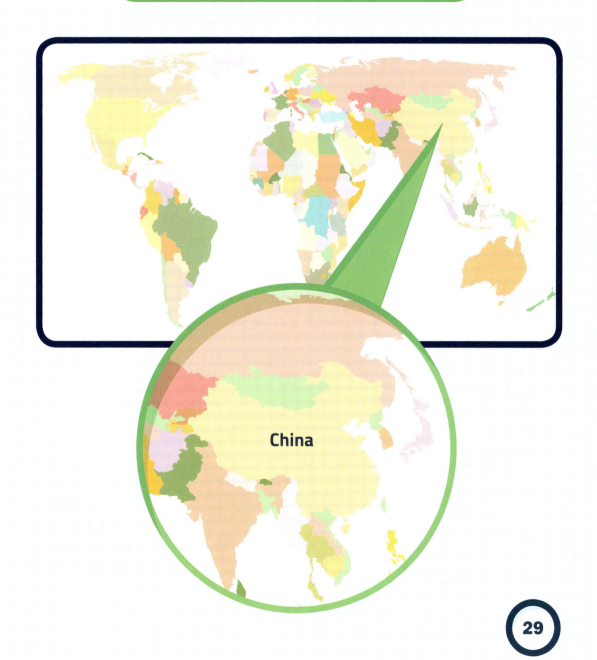

China

Glossary

atheist
A person or group who believes that God doesn't exist.

big data
Technologies that help organize and analyze huge amounts of facts and information.

communism
A social system where property and resources are owned by everyone rather than by individuals.

environment
Everything that is around us. Our surroundings.

ethnic group
A group of people who share the same culture, religion, and language.

government
The agency in charge of running a country.

infrastructure
The public system of transportation, energy, and communications of a country.

literate
Able to read and write.

party
A group of like-minded people organized to influence how a government is run.

pollute
To spoil a natural resource by making it unclean.

population
The number of all of the people living in an area.

province
A division of a country, like a state.

rural
From or in the country.

technology
The use of science to solve problems for practical purposes.

urban
From or in the city.

For More Information

Books

Colson, Mary. *Chinese Culture.* Global Cultures. North Mankato, MN: Capstone, 2013.

Jazynka, Kitson. *Mission: Panda Rescue: All About Pandas and How to Save Them.* Washington, DC: National Geographic Kids, 2016.

Kenney, Karen Latchana. *Mysteries of the Great Wall of China.* Ancient Mysteries. Minneapolis: Lerner Publishing Group, 2018.

Roberts, Jack L., and Michael M. Owens. *A Kid's Guide to China.* CreateSpace Independent Publishing Platform, 2017.

Visit 12StoryLibrary.com

Scan the code or use your school's login at **12StoryLibrary.com** for recent updates about this topic and a full digital version of this book. Enjoy free access to:

- Digital ebook
- Breaking news updates
- Live content feeds
- Videos, interactive maps, and graphics
- Additional web resources

Note to educators: Visit 12StoryLibrary.com/register to sign up for free premium website access. Enjoy live content plus a full digital version of every 12-Story Library book you own for every student at your school.

Index

About the Author

Marne Ventura has written over 50 children's books. A former elementary school teacher, Marne holds a master's degree in education from the University of California. She lives with her husband on the central coast of California.